THE VANCOUVER SUN

the best

salads

BY CANADA'S BEST-SELLING AUTHORS FROM *THE VANCOUVER SUN* TEST KITCHEN

RUTH PHELAN AND BRENDA THOMPSON

Published by Pacific Newspaper Group, A CanWest Company
1-200 Granville Street
Vancouver, B.C.
V6C 3N3

Pacific Newspaper Group President and Publisher:
  Dennis Skulsky

Library and Archives Canada Cataloguing in Publication

Phelan, Ruth, 1960-
  The best salads / Ruth Phelan and Brenda Thompson.

(The best cookbook series)
Includes index.
ISBN 0-9737410-7-4

  1. Salads. I. Thompson, Brenda, 1944- II. Title. III. Series: Best cookbook series

TX740.P49 2005   641.8'3   C2005-903334-7

All photographs by Peter Battistoni

Back cover photograph: CanWest Global Communications Corp.

Home Economists: Ruth Phelan & Brenda Thompson

Nutritional Analysis: Jean Fremont

Index: Lucia Jamieson

Edited by Shelley Fralic.

Printed and bound in Canada by Friesens

First Edition

10 9 8 7 6 5 4 3 2 1

Introduction

Take a crisp green lettuce and tear it into a large wooden bowl. Toss in your favourite fresh or leftover fixings, and drizzle with a tangy dressing — and the salad's ready.

But there's so much more to salads these days than fresh greens and cut vegetables. Everything imaginable is being tossed into the mix — from hot grilled vegetables, trendy chewy grains, interesting pastas and fresh and dried fruit to intensely flavoured cheese and buttery pine nuts.

Salads can be enjoyed on their own as a complete meal, or play the role of a good accompaniment to summer barbecued food or winter soups and stews.

This handy, purse-size cookbook is a collection of the best 50 salad recipes from *The Vancouver Sun* Test Kitchen (formerly known as *Edith Adams Cottage*). All 50 salad recipes — and four dressing recipes — were fine-tuned and taste tested until we were satisfied with the results. The good-enough-to-eat photographs were taken by *The Vancouver Sun* photographer Peter Battistoni.

We hope you'll enjoy making these five-star winners, from the second book in our *The Best* cookbook series.

Ruth Phelan
Brenda Thompson
Vancouver, B.C.
June 2005

A Cook's Guide to the Recipes

- Read the recipe from start to finish before you start to prepare ingredients. Ensure that you have all of the ingredients as well as the necessary equipment.

- All recipes use dried pasta unless specified otherwise. Although we give boiling times for dried pasta they may vary from brand to brand. Please follow the cooking times suggested on the package.

- Use medium-size fruit and vegetables unless specified otherwise.

- Parmesan cheese is freshly grated.

- Salt is regular table salt. Pepper is freshly ground black pepper.

- Lemon and lime juices are freshly squeezed, not bottled juice.

- Cook food uncovered unless specified otherwise.

- "Chicken breast" means a single (half) breast, not a double (whole) breast.

- Use pure sesame oil, not a blend of oils.

- To toast nuts, place nuts on rimmed baking sheet. Bake at 350 F (180 C) until fragrant and lightly browned — sliced natural almonds take about 5 minutes, pecans take 6 to 8 minutes and walnuts take 8 to 10 minutes.

- To toast hazelnuts, spread nuts on rimmed baking sheet and bake at 350 F (180 C) for 8 to 10 minutes or until fragrant and lightly browned. Transfer nuts to clean tea towel; roll nuts around, inside towel, to remove as much of the skins as possible. Let cool.

- To toast pine nuts, spread on rimmed baking sheet and bake at 325 F (160 C) for 5 to 8 minutes or until golden.

- To roast bell peppers, put peppers on baking sheet and broil for 20 to 25 minutes or until the skin is lightly charred, turning occasionally. Immediately place peppers in bowl and cover tightly with plastic wrap; let stand for 20 minutes. Peel, seed and devein peppers. *(Make ahead: Place prepared peppers in bowl; cover tightly with plastic wrap and refrigerate for up to 2 days.)*

Chicken Soba Noodle Salad (recipe on following page)

Mainly MEALS

Chicken Soba Noodle Salad

Vinaigrette

3   tablespoons (45 mL) soy sauce
1   tablespoon (15 mL) natural rice vinegar
1   tablespoon (15 mL) granulated sugar
3   tablespoons (45 mL) dark sesame oil
½   teaspoon (2 mL) hot chili oil

Salad

¾   pound (350 g) soba noodles
2   cups (500 mL) slivered cooked chicken
1   red bell pepper, sliced thin
6   green onions, sliced thin on the diagonal
2   carrots, grated
    Salt and pepper
    Toasted sesame seeds

Vinaigrette: In small bowl, whisk together soy sauce, vinegar and sugar. Gradually whisk in sesame oil and chili oil.

Salad: Cook noodles in large pot of boiling salted water until tender, according to package directions (watch cooking time — these noodles overcook quickly and become mushy); drain. Immediately rinse noodles under cold running water; drain well and put in large bowl.

Whisk vinaigrette and drizzle over noodles; toss to coat. Add chicken, bell pepper, two-thirds of the green onions and half the carrots; toss. Add salt and pepper to taste. Transfer to platter and sprinkle with remaining onions and carrots. Sprinkle with sesame seeds.

Tips:

• *Different brands of chili oil vary in heat intensity. Taste the vinaigrette and increase the chili oil if you like your food really hot.*

• *Resembling spaghetti but slightly shorter, soba noodles (also called buckwheat noodles) range in colour from beige to dark brown. They're made from 100-per-cent buckwheat flour, or a combination of buckwheat and wheat flours.*

• *If your package of soba noodles doesn't have cooking instructions, simply drop noodles into large pot of boiling salted water and simmer for about 6 to 9 minutes or until tender.*

• *To measure soba noodles: Grasp a handful of noodles tightly at one end, then measure the diameter. If it's about 2-inches (5 cm) across, you have about three-quarters of a pound (350 g).*

• *Make ahead: Cook noodles the day before serving and add vinaigrette; cover tightly and refrigerate overnight. Before serving, remove noodles from fridge and let come to room temperature. The final assembly will take just a few minutes.*

• *When you're cooking chicken breasts for dinner, add an extra large whole breast and you'll have enough to make this salad the next day.*

Makes 4 servings. PER SERVING: 545 cal, 33 g pro, 16 g fat, 72 g carb.

Grilled Salmon and Pecan Salad

Grilled Salmon

2	tablespoons (30 mL) olive oil
3	tablespoons (45 mL) fresh lemon juice
2	large garlic cloves, crushed
4	salmon fillets (skinless), about 6 ounces (170 g) each

Vinaigrette

2	tablespoons (30 mL) apple cider vinegar
½	teaspoon (2 mL) each salt and pepper
¼	cup (50 mL) hazelnut oil
3	tablespoons (45 mL) chopped fresh basil

Salad

8	cups (2 L) torn mixed sturdy salad greens
½	cup (125 mL) pecans, toasted and chopped coarse
	Salt and pepper

Grilled Salmon: In small bowl, gradually whisk oil into lemon juice. Whisk in garlic; remove 2 tablespoons (30 mL) for basting and set aside. Put remaining lemon-oil mixture in shallow glass baking dish large enough to hold salmon fillets in single layer. Add fillets, turning to coat evenly; let stand for 5 minutes.

Vinaigrette: In small bowl, whisk together vinegar, salt and pepper. Gradually whisk in oil. Whisk in basil.

Salad: In large bowl, combine greens and pecans.

Put fillets in well-greased, hinged, wire rack holder. Place on barbecue grill over medium-high heat. Cook fish for 10 minutes per inch (2.5 cm) of thickness or until fish flakes easily when tested with a fork, turning once and basting occasionally with reserved lemon-oil mixture.

Whisk vinaigrette and drizzle over greens mixture; toss to coat. Place an equal portion of greens mixture on each of 4 plates. Cut each fillet in half. Place 2 salmon pieces, one slightly overlapping the other, on top of each plate of greens. Sprinkle with salt and pepper to taste.

Tip: *A 283-gram package of washed, ready-to-use European salad blend (iceberg, romaine and green leaf lettuce, plus radicchio and endive) contains about 8 cups (2 L) torn greens.*

Makes 4 servings. PER SERVING: 505 cal, 37 g pro, 37 g fat, 8 g carb.

Cobb Salad

Vinaigrette

1½ tablespoons (22 mL) red wine vinegar

1 teaspoon (5 mL) dijon mustard

¼ teaspoon (1 mL) each salt and pepper

⅓ cup (75 mL) olive oil

1 garlic clove, minced

1 tablespoon (15 mL) finely chopped shallot

Salad

4 cups (1 L) sliced (½-inch/1 cm wide) romaine lettuce

6 slices bacon, cooked crisp and crumbled

3 hard-cooked eggs, cut into wedges

2 large tomatoes, cored, seeded and chopped coarse

1½ cups (375 mL) cubed cooked chicken or turkey breast

2 cups (500 mL) coarsely chopped watercress leaves

½ cup (125 mL) crumbled blue cheese

½ small red onion, sliced thin

Vinaigrette: In small bowl, whisk together vinegar, mustard, salt and pepper. Gradually whisk in oil. Whisk in garlic and shallot.

Salad: Line platter with lettuce. Arrange bacon, eggs, tomatoes, chicken, watercress, cheese and onion in narrow rows on top of lettuce. Whisk vinaigrette and drizzle 2 tablespoons (30 mL) over salad. Serve remaining vinaigrette separately.

Tip: *You think you know how to "boil" an egg? Here's the foolproof way: Put eggs into saucepan; cover with cold water and put over high heat. Bring to a boil. Remove pan from heat, cover and let stand for 20 minutes; drain. Put eggs under cold running water until chilled. Crack shells by tapping on counter; then peel under cold running water.*

Makes 6 servings. PER SERVING: 328 cal, 26 g pro, 22 g fat, 6 g carb.

Sauteed Oysters on Bed of Greens

Vinaigrette

1½	tablespoons (22 mL) white balsamic vinegar
1	tablespoon (15 mL) white wine vinegar
½	teaspoon (2 mL) dijon mustard
¼	teaspoon (1 mL) liquid honey
¼	teaspoon (1 mL) each salt and pepper
2	tablespoons (30 mL) olive oil
2	tablespoons (30 mL) finely chopped shallot

Salad

12	cups (3 L) torn mixed sturdy salad greens
1	red bell pepper, cut into thin strips
3	slices bacon
	Salt and pepper

Oysters

⅓	cup (75 mL) all-purpose flour
⅓	cup (75 mL) yellow cornmeal
¼	teaspoon (1 mL) each salt and pepper
⅛	teaspoon (0.5 mL) cayenne pepper
2	(227 g) containers shucked fresh Pacific oysters
1	tablespoon (15 mL) butter

Vinaigrette: In small bowl, whisk together balsamic and wine vinegars, mustard, honey, salt and pepper. Gradually whisk in oil. Whisk in shallot.

Salad: In large bowl, combine greens and bell pepper. In large heavy frypan, saute bacon over medium heat until crisp. Transfer bacon to paper-towel-lined plate (do not discard bacon fat); crumble bacon and set aside.

Oysters: Combine flour, cornmeal, salt, pepper and cayenne pepper in pie plate. Drain and pat oysters dry with paper towel; cut any large ones in half. Add oysters to flour mixture; toss to coat.

Using same frypan, add butter to bacon fat and heat over medium-high heat. Add oysters and saute for 2 minutes or until cooked and golden brown, turning once; set aside.

To assemble: Whisk vinaigrette and drizzle over greens mixture; toss to coat. Place an equal portion of greens mixture on each of 4 plates. Top each with an equal portion of sauteed oysters and bacon. Sprinkle with salt and pepper to taste.

Tip: Sturdy greens are the best choice for warm salads as they tend to stand up to the hot ingredients that are placed on top. A mixture of iceberg, romaine and green leaf lettuce plus radicchio and endive would be a good choice, as they can withstand a little heat. Add just a few tender baby greens, if desired.

Makes 4 servings. PER SERVING: 530 cal, 25 g pro, 28 g fat, 52 g carb.

Grilled Chicken Salad

Dressing

2	tablespoons (30 mL) white wine vinegar
2	tablespoons (30 mL) liquid honey
2	tablespoons (30 mL) light mayonnaise
½	teaspoon (2 mL) dijon mustard
1	large garlic clove, minced
¼	teaspoon (1 mL) each salt and pepper
½	cup (125 mL) olive oil
1	tablespoon (15 mL) finely chopped fresh basil

Salad

4	boneless skinless chicken breasts
1	tablespoon (15 mL) olive oil
	Salt and pepper
8	cups (2 L) torn mixed sturdy salad greens
¾	cup (175 mL) halved grape or cherry tomatoes
¼	cup (50 mL) sliced green onions
	Salt and pepper

Dressing: In small bowl, whisk together vinegar, honey, mayonnaise, mustard, garlic, salt and pepper. Gradually whisk in oil. Whisk in basil.

Salad: Pound chicken breasts until ½-inch (1 cm) thick. Brush with oil; sprinkle with salt and pepper. Place chicken on greased barbecue grill over medium-high heat and cook for 8 minutes or until no longer pink inside, turning once. Cut chicken into thin slices.

Place an equal portion of greens on each of 4 plates. Top each with an equal portion of tomatoes and hot chicken. Sprinkle each salad with 1 tablespoon (15 mL) onion. Whisk dressing and drizzle each salad with one-quarter of the dressing. Sprinkle with salt and pepper to taste.

Tip: Fresh Italian (flat-leaf) parsley can be substituted for fresh basil.

Makes 4 servings. PER SERVING: 486 cal, 29 g pro, 36 g fat, 14 g carb.

Spicy Pasta Salad with Prawns

Salad

¾ pound (350 g) spaghetti or linguine

¼ pound (125 g) snow peas, trimmed (1 cup/250 mL)

¾ pound (350 g) shelled cooked prawns (about 28)

4 green onions, sliced diagonally

1½ cups (375 mL) bean sprouts

¼ cup (50 mL) chopped fresh cilantro

Salt and pepper

Dressing

3 tablespoons (45 mL) smooth natural peanut butter

3 tablespoons (45 mL) soy sauce

3 tablespoons (45 mL) natural rice vinegar

4 teaspoons (20 mL) vegetable oil

4 teaspoons (20 mL) grated fresh ginger

¼ teaspoon (1 mL) dried crushed hot red pepper

Salad: Cook spaghetti in large pot of boiling salted water for 10 minutes or until tender, adding peas during the last 1 minute of cooking time; drain. Immediately rinse pasta and peas under cold running water; drain well and put in large bowl. Add prawns, onions, bean sprouts and cilantro.

Dressing: In small bowl, whisk together peanut butter, soy sauce and vinegar. In small saucepan, heat oil over medium-high heat. Add ginger and dried red pepper; cook for 1 minute. Remove pan from heat and add peanut butter mixture; whisk until smooth. Drizzle over salad; toss to coat. Add salt and pepper to taste. Transfer to platter.

Tip: Use natural peanut butter instead of homogenized peanut butter.

Makes 4 servings. PER SERVING: 552 cal, 35 g pro, 13 g fat, 73 g carb.

Mediterranean Orzo and Tuna Salad

Vinaigrette

2	tablespoons (30 mL) white wine vinegar
¾	teaspoon (4 mL) dijon mustard
¼	teaspoon (1 mL) liquid honey
¾	teaspoon (4 mL) salt
¼	teaspoon (1 mL) pepper
½	cup (125 mL) olive oil
2	tablespoons (30 mL) chopped, drained sun-dried tomatoes (packed in oil)
2	garlic cloves, minced
1	tablespoon (15 mL) finely chopped shallot
1	tablespoon (15 mL) chopped fresh basil

Salad

1¾	cups (425 mL) orzo (rice-shaped pasta)
½	pound (250 g) sugar snap peas, trimmed (2 cups/500 mL)
1	(170 mL) jar marinated artichoke hearts, drained and chopped coarse
1	(398 mL) can black beans, drained and rinsed
1	(170 g) can solid white tuna (packed in water), drained and separated into small chunks
1	small red bell pepper, diced
⅓	cup (75 mL) chopped red onion
¼	cup (50 mL) sliced, pitted green olives
¼	cup (50 mL) pine nuts, toasted
⅓	cup (75 mL) chopped fresh parsley
2	cups (500 mL) grape or cherry tomatoes, halved
	Salt and pepper

Vinaigrette: In small bowl, whisk together vinegar, mustard, honey, salt and pepper. Gradually whisk in oil. Whisk in sun-dried tomatoes, garlic, shallot and basil.

Salad: Cook orzo in large pot of boiling salted water for 10 minutes or until tender, adding peas during last 1 minute of cooking time; drain. Immediately rinse pasta and peas under cold running water; drain well and put in large bowl. Add artichoke hearts, beans, tuna, bell pepper, onion, olives, pine nuts and parsley; toss to combine. Add tomatoes; toss gently.

Drizzle vinaigrette over salad; toss to coat. Add salt and pepper to taste. Transfer to platter.

Tips:

• *Pick up your favourite green olives — we like hot Sicilian or Spanish olives. Green olives generally contain less oil and have a sharper flavour and firmer flesh than black olives.*

• *A 250-gram package of washed, ready-to-use fresh, stringless sugar snap peas yields about 2 cups (500 mL).*

Makes 6 servings. PER SERVING: 465 cal, 20 g pro, 25 g fat, 44 g carb.

Cucumber and Pepper Salad Pizza

Vinaigrette

2	tablespoons (30 mL) olive oil
2	teaspoons (10 mL) sherry vinegar

Pizza

2½	cups (625 mL) grated fontina or provolone cheese
2	(12-inch/30 cm) store-bought, prebaked thin pizza crusts
½	cup (125 mL) thinly sliced red onion
½	cup (125 mL) walnuts, chopped coarse
2	garlic cloves, minced
½	teaspoon (2 mL) olive oil
2	ounces (60 g) prosciutto, chopped coarse
6	cups (1.5 L) torn mixed salad greens
¼	cup (50 mL) crumbled blue cheese
½	cup (125 mL) halved grape or cherry tomatoes
1	mini cucumber, sliced or ½ cup (125 mL) sliced English cucumber
1	yellow sweetooth or small bell pepper, sliced
	Coarsely ground pepper

Vinaigrette: In small bowl, gradually whisk oil into vinegar.

Pizza: For each pizza: Sprinkle half the fontina cheese evenly over pizza crust. Arrange half the onion and walnuts on top. Sprinkle with half the garlic. Bake at 450 F (230 C) for 10 minutes or until cheese is melted.

Meanwhile, heat oil in medium-size heavy frypan over medium heat. Add prosciutto and saute for 3 minutes or until crisp.

Top hot pizza with half the greens. Sprinkle evenly with half the blue cheese. Top with half the tomatoes, cucumber and yellow pepper. Whisk vinaigrette and drizzle half over pizza. Sprinkle with half the prosciutto. Sprinkle with pepper to taste. Makes 2 pizzas.

Makes 4 servings. PER SERVING: 1,080 cal, 42 g pro, 46 g fat, 124 g carb.

Greek Pasta Salad

Vinaigrette

4	teaspoons (20 mL) red wine vinegar
4	teaspoons (20 mL) fresh lemon juice
½	teaspoon (2 mL) salt
¼	teaspoon (1 mL) pepper
¼	cup (50 mL) olive oil
1	large garlic clove, minced
⅛	teaspoon (0.5 mL) dried oregano leaves

Salad

3	cups (750 mL) tortiglioni pasta
1	(540 mL) can chickpeas, drained and rinsed
2	cups (500 mL) bite-size pieces English cucumber
2	cups (500 mL) cherry tomatoes, quartered
1	green bell pepper, cut into bite-size pieces
1½	cups (375 mL) crumbled feta cheese
½	cup (125 mL) pitted kalamata olives
⅓	cup (75 mL) chopped fresh Italian (flat-leaf) parsley
	Salt and pepper

Vinaigrette: In small bowl, whisk together vinegar, lemon juice, salt and pepper. Gradually whisk in oil. Whisk in garlic and oregano.

Salad: Cook tortiglioni in large pot of boiling salted water for 8 minutes or until tender; drain. Immediately rinse pasta under cold running water; drain well and put in large bowl. Add chickpeas, cucumber, tomatoes, bell pepper, cheese, olives and parsley. Whisk vinaigrette and drizzle over salad; toss to coat. Add salt and pepper to taste.

Tip: Tortiglioni are large spiral-edged tubes of pasta. You can substitute scoobi doo or fusilli pasta.

Makes 6 servings. PER SERVING: 556 cal, 21 g pro, 28 g fat, 57 g carb.

Tuscan Bread Salad

Vinaigrette
3   tablespoons (45 mL) red wine vinegar
½   teaspoon (2 mL) dijon mustard
½   teaspoon (2 mL) each salt and pepper
6   tablespoons (90 mL) olive oil

Salad
1   garlic clove, minced
2   tablespoons (30 mL) olive oil
½   sourdough baguette, cut in half lengthwise
⅓   cup (75 mL) pine nuts
1   (398 mL) can red kidney beans, drained and rinsed
3   large ripe tomatoes, cut into chunks
2   cups (500 mL) cubed English cucumber
½   cup (125 mL) diced feta cheese
⅓   cup (75 mL) currants
½   cup (125 mL) chopped fresh Italian (flat-leaf) parsley
⅓   cup (75 mL) chopped fresh basil
     Salt and pepper

Vinaigrette: In small bowl, whisk together vinegar, mustard, salt and pepper. Gradually whisk in oil.

Salad: In small bowl, stir together garlic and oil; brush over cut sides of baguette. Cut into ¾-inch (2 cm) chunks (6 cups/1.5 L); put on rimmed baking sheet. Bake at 350 F (180 C) for 13 minutes or until bread is golden, adding pine nuts during last 5 minutes of baking time. Let cool.

In large bowl, combine beans, tomatoes, cucumber, cheese, currants, parsley, basil, toasted bread and pine nuts. Whisk vinaigrette and drizzle over salad; toss to coat. Add salt and pepper to taste.

Tip: Use chewy-textured baguette: Ordinary bread turns mushy.

Makes 4 servings. PER SERVING: 639 cal, 19 g pro, 43 g fat, 50 g carb.

Warm Taco Salad

8	cups (2 L) shredded romaine or iceberg lettuce
4	cups (1 L) tortilla chips
4½	cups (1.125 L) home-made or store-bought ground beef chili, heated
1	cup (250 mL) chopped tomato
1	cup (250 mL) finely grated cheddar cheese
4	tablespoons (60 mL) light sour cream
	Chopped green onion or fresh cilantro, optional

Place an equal portion of lettuce on each of 4 plates. Arrange 1 cup (250 mL) tortilla chips around edge of each plate. Spoon one-quarter of the hot chili on top of each plate of lettuce. Top each with one-quarter of the tomato, cheese and sour cream; sprinkle with onion.

Tip: *To save preparation time, buy canned chili, grated cheese and packaged washed lettuce.*

Makes 4 servings. PER SERVING: 633 cal, 32 g pro, 33 g fat, 55 g carb.

Grilled Salmon with Mango-Raspberry Spinach Salad

½   cup (125 mL) store-bought raspberry vinaigrette
2   tablespoons (30 mL) finely chopped shallot
4   salmon steaks, about 6 ounces (170 g) each
    Salt and pepper
1   red onion, cut into ¼-inch (5 mm) thick slices
8   cups (2 L) lightly packed fresh baby spinach
1   mango, sliced thin
1   cup (250 mL) fresh raspberries, optional

In small bowl, whisk together vinaigrette and shallot; divide in half. Reserve half to toss with salad; use remaining half for grilling salmon.

Lightly sprinkle salmon steaks with salt and pepper. Skewer onion slices with toothpicks so they don't fall apart on the grill. Brush one side of steaks and onion slices with some of the vinaigrette reserved for grilling. Place steaks and onions, brushed side down, on greased barbecue grill over medium-high heat. Brush top of steaks and onion slices with remaining vinaigrette reserved for grilling. Cook fish for 10 minutes per inch (2.5 cm) of thickness or until fish flakes easily when tested with a fork and onion is tender-crisp, turning steaks and onion slices once.

In large bowl, combine spinach, mango and raspberries. Add grilled onion (toothpicks removed) and reserved vinaigrette; toss to coat. Place an equal portion of salad on each of 4 plates. Top each with a salmon steak.

Tip: *If desired, use ½ cup (125 mL) home-made Fresh Berry Vinaigrette (page 92) in place of store-bought vinaigrette and omit the 2 tablespoons (30 mL) shallot in salad recipe.*

Makes 4 servings. PER SERVING: 459 cal, 36 g pro, 28 g fat, 17 g carb.

Blood Orange Salad (recipe on following page)

Mainly GREENS

Blood Orange Salad

Vinaigrette

¼	cup (50 mL) blood orange juice
1½	tablespoons (22 mL) white balsamic vinegar
½	teaspoon (2 mL) liquid honey
¼	teaspoon (1 mL) dijon mustard
¼	teaspoon (1 mL) salt
	Pinch pepper
¼	cup (50 mL) olive oil
1	tablespoon (15 mL) finely chopped shallot

Salad

1	small fennel bulb
8	cups (2 L) torn mixed sturdy salad greens
2	cups (500 mL) watercress sprigs
3	blood oranges, sectioned and drained well
½	cup (125 mL) shaved parmesan cheese

Vinaigrette: In small bowl, whisk together orange juice, vinegar, honey, mustard, salt and pepper. Gradually whisk in oil. Whisk in shallot.

Salad: Cut fennel in half lengthwise; core and cut crosswise into very thin slices. In large bowl, combine fennel, greens and watercress.

Whisk vinaigrette and drizzle over greens mixture; toss to coat. Place an equal portion of greens mixture in each of 6 bowls; top each with an equal portion of orange sections and cheese.

Tip: Moro oranges, also known as blood oranges because of their sparkling maroon flesh, are slightly smaller than navel oranges, have a plum-like blush on the peel and few, if any, seeds. This eye-catching fruit has a rich, juicy orange taste with a hint of raspberry flavour that lingers on your tongue. Navel oranges can be substituted for blood oranges.

Makes 6 servings. PER SERVING: 153 cal, 6 g pro, 11 g fat, 9 g carb.

Caesar Salad

Croutons

2   cups (500 mL) ½-inch (1 cm) bread cubes

1   tablespoon (15 mL) olive oil

Vinaigrette

1   tablespoon (15 mL) fresh lemon juice

1   teaspoon (5 mL) red wine vinegar

2   teaspoons (10 mL) dijon mustard

1   teaspoon (5 mL) anchovy paste (optional)

1   teaspoon (5 mL) worcestershire sauce

¼   teaspoon (1 mL) each salt and pepper

⅓   cup (75 mL) olive oil

3   garlic cloves, minced

⅓   cup (75 mL) grated parmesan cheese

Salad

9   cups (2.25 L) torn romaine lettuce

   Salt and pepper

⅓   cup (75 mL) shaved or grated parmesan cheese

Croutons: In large bowl, toss bread cubes with oil. Spread on baking sheet. Bake at 350 F (180 C) for 10 to 12 minutes or until golden.

Vinaigrette: In small bowl, whisk together lemon juice, vinegar, mustard, anchovy paste, worcestershire sauce, salt and pepper. Gradually whisk in oil. Whisk in garlic and grated cheese.

Salad: In large bowl, combine lettuce and croutons. Whisk dressing and drizzle over salad; toss to coat. Add salt and pepper to taste. Sprinkle with shaved cheese.

Tip: *For creamy dressing, substitute ⅓ cup (75 mL) light mayonnaise for oil.*

Makes 4 servings. PER SERVING: 365 cal, 11 g pro, 26 g fat, 23 g carb.

Summer Tossed Salad
with Fig Balsamic Vinaigrette

Vinaigrette

2   tablespoons (30 mL) fig balsamic vinegar
½   teaspoon (2 mL) dijon mustard
¼   teaspoon (1 mL) salt
⅛   teaspoon (0.5 mL) pepper
¼   cup (50 mL) olive oil
1   small garlic clove, minced
1   tablespoon (15 mL) finely chopped shallot
2   tablespoons (30 mL) chopped fresh Italian (flat-leaf) parsley

Salad

10   cups (2.5 L) torn mixed salad greens
½   cup (125 mL) sliced radishes
2   mini cucumbers, sliced
2   green onions, sliced thin on the diagonal
2   tomatoes, cut into wedges
1   red sweetooth pepper, sliced crosswise
1   yellow sweetooth pepper, sliced crosswise
        Salt and pepper

Vinaigrette: In small bowl, whisk together vinegar, mustard, salt and pepper. Gradually whisk in oil. Whisk in garlic, shallot and parsley.

Salad: In large bowl, combine greens, radishes, cucumbers, onions, tomatoes, and red and yellow peppers.

Whisk vinaigrette and drizzle over salad; toss to coat. Add salt and pepper to taste.

Tips:

• *Substitute 1 cup (250 mL) sliced English cucumber for 2 mini cucumbers.*

• *Sweetooth super sweet peppers are newcomers to green grocer shelves. Sweeter tasting than the more squat-shaped bell peppers, their elongated shape, about 8 inches (20 cm), makes them perfect for slicing crosswise into attractive rings. If you can't find sweetooth peppers substitute 1 small bell pepper (sliced lengthwise) for 1 sweetooth pepper.*

• *Fig balsamic vinegar imparts an intense flavour boost while adding a delightful sweetness and fig aroma. Use the same amount of regular balsamic vinegar if you can't find fig balsamic vinegar — but check delis and specialty food stores first. Shake bottle before using.*

Makes 8 servings. PER SERVING: 69 cal, 1 g pro, 6 g fat, 4 g carb.

Strawberry Spinach Salad

Sugared almonds

½ cup (125 mL) slivered almonds
¼ cup (50 mL) granulated sugar
1 tablespoon (15 mL) water

Vinaigrette

4 teaspoons (20 mL) balsamic vinegar
2 teaspoons (10 mL) worcestershire sauce
2 teaspoons (10 mL) liquid honey
1¼ teaspoons (6 mL) poppy seeds
2 teaspoons (10 mL) finely chopped fresh chives
¼ teaspoon (1 mL) salt
⅛ teaspoon (0.5 mL) pepper
3 tablespoons (45 mL) olive oil

Salad

8 cups (2 L) fresh baby spinach
2 cups (500 mL) sliced strawberries
Salt and pepper

Sugared almonds: In medium saucepan, combine almonds, sugar and water. Cook over medium-low heat for 5 to 10 minutes or until sugar is almost completely melted and nuts are golden, stirring constantly (there will be a few grains of unmelted sugar on nuts). Spread nuts on baking sheet; let cool and break into small pieces.

Vinaigrette: In small bowl, whisk together vinegar, worcestershire sauce, honey, seeds, chives, salt and pepper. Gradually whisk in oil.

Salad: In large bowl, combine spinach and strawberries. Whisk vinaigrette and drizzle over salad; toss gently to coat. Add nuts; toss gently. Add salt and pepper to taste.

Tip: *For a main course, add ½ pound (250 g) slivered cooked chicken or turkey.*

Makes 6 servings. PER SERVING: 190 cal, 4 g pro, 13 g fat, 17 g carb.

Greens with Cherry Vinaigrette

Vinaigrette

2½	tablespoons (37 mL) cherry vinegar
¼	teaspoon (1 mL) grainy mustard
⅛	teaspoon (0.5 mL) granulated sugar
⅛	teaspoon (0.5 mL) each salt and pepper
¼	cup (50 mL) olive oil
1	tablespoon (15 mL) finely chopped shallot

Salad

½	teaspoon (2 mL) olive oil
2	ounces (60 g) prosciutto, chopped coarse
2	pears, cored and sliced
	Fresh lemon juice
6	cups (1.5 L) torn mixed salad greens
½	cup (125 mL) dried sweet cherries, halved
½	cup (125 mL) hazelnuts, toasted and chopped coarse

Vinaigrette: In small bowl, whisk together vinegar, mustard, sugar, salt and pepper. Gradually whisk in oil. Whisk in shallot.

Salad: In medium-size heavy frypan, heat oil over medium heat. Add prosciutto and saute for 3 minutes or until crisp.

Brush pear slices with lemon juice. In large bowl, combine greens, cherries, hazelnuts, pears and prosciutto. Whisk vinaigrette and drizzle over salad; toss to coat.

Tip: You'll probably have to check specialty food stores in your neighbourhood to find cherry vinegar, but it's worth the effort. Although you could substitute a good quality white wine vinegar, it won't impart the delicate fruity flavour that the cherry vinegar does so well.

Makes 4 servings. PER SERVING: 342 cal, 7 g pro, 24 g fat, 30 g carb.

Mixed Greens with Mango and Pomegranate Seeds

Vinaigrette

3	tablespoons (45 mL) pomegranate balsamic vinegar
1	teaspoon (5 mL) grainy mustard
¼	teaspoon (1 mL) salt
⅛	teaspoon (0.5 mL) pepper
¼	cup (50 mL) olive oil
2	tablespoons (30 mL) finely sliced fresh chives or green onion

Salad

12	cups (3 L) torn mixed salad greens
2	cups (500 mL) bite-size pieces radicchio leaves
2	mangoes, cubed
½	red onion, sliced thin
½	cup (125 mL) sliced natural almonds, toasted
½	cup (125 mL) pomegranate seeds
	Salt and pepper

Vinaigrette: In small bowl, whisk together vinegar, mustard, salt and pepper. Gradually whisk in oil. Whisk in chives.

Salad: In large bowl, combine greens, radicchio, mangoes and onion. Whisk vinaigrette and drizzle over greens mixture; toss to coat. Add almonds and pomegranate seeds, toss gently. Add salt and pepper to taste.

Tip: *Pomegranate balsamic vinegar is sweet. Regular balsamic vinegar can be substituted for this fruit vinegar: Reduce regular balsamic vinegar to 2 tablespoons (30 mL) and add ½ teaspoon (2 mL) granulated sugar.*

Makes 8 servings. PER SERVING: 159 cal, 3 g pro, 10 g fat, 16 g carb.

Moroccan Orange Salad

Vinaigrette

3	tablespoons (45 mL) fresh orange juice
½	teaspoon (2 mL) dijon mustard
½	teaspoon (2 mL) liquid honey
¼	teaspoon (1 mL) salt
⅛	teaspoon (0.5 mL) pepper
1	tablespoon (15 mL) olive oil
1	garlic clove, minced
1	small serrano pepper, seeded and minced
1	teaspoon (5 mL) finely grated orange zest

Salad

8	cups (2 L) lightly packed arugula leaves
3	large navel oranges
½	small red onion, sliced thin
½	cup (125 mL) slivered pitted medjool dates
⅓	cup (75 mL) unsalted natural pistachios, chopped coarse
¼	cup (50 mL) Moroccan black olives
	Salt and pepper

Vinaigrette: In small bowl, whisk together orange juice, mustard, honey, salt and pepper. Gradually whisk in oil. Whisk in garlic, serrano pepper and zest.

Salad: Line platter with arugula. Peel oranges and cut into ¼-inch (5 mm) thick slices. Arrange oranges and onion on top of arugula. Sprinkle with dates, pistachios and olives. Whisk vinaigrette and drizzle over salad. Sprinkle with salt and pepper to taste.

Tip: Whole medjool dates are big, plump and very moist. Look for them in the produce section, sold either in bulk or in plastic containers.

Makes 8 servings. PER SERVING: 118 cal, 2 g pro, 5 g fat, 19 g carb.

Spinach and Goat Cheese Salad

Vinaigrette

3	tablespoons (45 mL) white balsamic vinegar
½	teaspoon (2 mL) dijon mustard
½	teaspoon (2 mL) salt
⅛	teaspoon (0.5 mL) pepper
3	tablespoons (45 mL) olive oil
1	tablespoon (15 mL) finely chopped shallot

Salad

½	teaspoon (2 mL) olive oil
2	ounces (60 g) prosciutto, chopped coarse
1	Asian pear or apple, cored and sliced
	Fresh lemon juice
12	cups (3 L) torn spinach leaves
¼	cup (50 mL) unripened soft goat cheese, cut into small pieces
	Salt and pepper
⅓	cup (75 mL) hazelnuts, toasted and chopped coarse

Vinaigrette: In small bowl, whisk together vinegar, mustard, salt and pepper. Gradually whisk in oil. Whisk in shallot.

Salad: In medium-size heavy frypan, heat oil over medium heat. Add prosciutto and saute for 3 minutes or until crisp.

Cut pear slices in half and lightly brush with lemon juice. In large bowl, combine spinach, cheese, prosciutto and pear slices.

Whisk vinaigrette and drizzle over salad; toss to coat. Add salt and pepper to taste. Sprinkle with hazelnuts.

Tip: A 283-gram package of spinach yields about 12 cups (3 L) lightly packed.

Makes 8 servings. PER SERVING: 137 cal, 5 g pro, 11 g fat, 7 g carb.

Wheat Berry Salad (recipe on following page)

Mainly GRAINS

Wheat Berry Salad

Salad

1	cup (250 mL) wheat berries
	Salt
¼	pound (125 g) snow peas, trimmed (1 cup/250 mL)
1	small red bell pepper, cut into small pieces
⅓	cup (75 mL) chopped red onion
½	cup (125 mL) dried sweet cherries, halved
½	cup (125 mL) chopped fresh Italian (flat-leaf) parsley
1	tablespoon (15 mL) chopped fresh basil
	Pepper

Vinaigrette

1½	tablespoons (22 mL) cider vinegar
1	teaspoon (5 mL) grainy mustard
¼	teaspoon (1 mL) each salt and pepper
3	tablespoons (45 mL) olive oil
1	tablespoon (15 mL) finely chopped shallot

Salad: In medium saucepan, bring 4 cups (1 L) water to a boil over medium-high heat. Add wheat berries and ¾ teaspoon (4 mL) salt; reduce heat and simmer, covered, for 1½ to 2 hours or until wheat berries are tender. (Once the berries begin to split, stop cooking.) Drain and let cool to room temperature (about 1 hour), stirring occasionally.

Meanwhile, cook peas in medium saucepan of boiling water for 1 minute or until tender-crisp; drain. Immediately rinse under cold running water; drain well. Cut peas in half diagonally.

In large bowl, combine wheat berries, peas, bell pepper, onion, cherries, parsley and basil.

Vinaigrette: In small bowl, whisk together vinegar, mustard, salt and pepper. Gradually whisk in oil. Whisk in shallot.

Drizzle vinaigrette over salad; toss to coat. Add salt and pepper to taste.

Tips:

• *Look for wheat berries, the unprocessed whole soft or hard wheat kernels, at natural food stores. The more difficult to find, soft wheat berries, take less time to cook than the hard wheat berries.*
• *Cooked wheat berries have a pleasant, nutty flavour and chewy texture. The cooking time of wheat berries can be reduced by about 30 minutes by soaking the kernels overnight in cold water.*

Makes 4 servings. PER SERVING: 324 cal, 10 g pro, 12 g fat, 50 g carb.

White Bean Salad with Warm Sherry Vinegar Dressing

Salad

2   (398 mL) cans navy beans, drained and rinsed
1   large red or yellow bell pepper, roasted and cut into thin strips
⅓   cup (75 mL) chopped fresh Italian (flat-leaf) parsley
     Salt and pepper

Dressing

5   tablespoons (75 mL) olive oil, divided
⅓   cup (75 mL) chopped red onion
3   ounces (90 g) prosciutto, chopped coarse
1   large garlic clove, minced
3   tablespoons (45 mL) sherry vinegar or red wine vinegar

Salad: In large bowl, combine beans and bell pepper.

Dressing: In medium-size heavy frypan, heat 1 tablespoon (15 mL) oil over medium heat. Add onion and saute for 1 minute. Add prosciutto and garlic; saute for 3 minutes or until onion is tender. Remove pan from heat; stir in vinegar and remaining 4 tablespoons (60 mL) oil. Immediately pour over bean mixture; stir to coat. Add parsley, and salt and pepper to taste. Transfer to platter.

Tips:

• *Any small white bean will do — navy, great northern and white kidney beans are all suitable for this gutsy wine vinegar dressing.*
• *Time saver: Use ½ cup (125 mL) drained, bottled roasted bell pepper strips instead of roasting a fresh pepper. The peppers come whole in a jar; remove 1 or 2 and simply cut into strips.*

Makes 6 servings. PER SERVING: 246 cal, 11 g pro, 13 g fat, 24 g carb.

Fattoush

Vinaigrette

¼   cup (50 mL) fresh lemon juice
¼   teaspoon (1 mL) each salt and pepper
¼   cup (50 mL) olive oil
2   garlic cloves, minced

Salad

2   pita breads
2   cups (500 mL) grape or cherry tomatoes, halved
1   cup (250 mL) shredded romaine lettuce
1   cup (250 mL) sliced green onions
⅓   cup (75 mL) pitted Lebanese or kalamata olives, halved
2   mini cucumbers, sliced
1   small yellow bell pepper, cut into bite-size pieces
½   cup (125 mL) chopped fresh Italian (flat-leaf) parsley
¼   cup (50 mL) chopped fresh mint
3   tablespoons (45 mL) chopped fresh cilantro
    Salt and pepper

Vinaigrette: In small bowl, whisk together lemon juice, salt and pepper. Gradually whisk in oil. Whisk in garlic.

Salad: Horizontally split pita breads in half; place on baking sheet. Bake at 350 F (180 C) for 5 minutes or until crisp. Break into bite-size pieces.

Meanwhile, combine tomatoes, lettuce, onions, olives, cucumbers, bell pepper, parsley, mint and cilantro in large bowl. Whisk vinaigrette and drizzle over salad; toss to coat. Stir in crisp pita bread pieces. Add salt and pepper to taste.

Tip: To prevent crisp pita bread from becoming too soggy, toss into this Lebanese-inspired salad just before serving.

Makes 4 servings. PER SERVING: 270 cal, 6 g pro, 16 g fat, 29 g carb.

Navy Bean Salad
with Grilled Vegetables

Vinaigrette

4½ tablespoons (67 mL) olive oil
3 tablespoons (45 mL) white wine vinegar
3 tablespoons (45 mL) finely chopped fresh basil
1 tablespoon (15 mL) finely chopped fresh sage
1 teaspoon (5 mL) finely chopped fresh rosemary

Salad

2 (398 mL) cans navy beans, drained and rinsed
3 cups (750 mL) sliced green beans (1½ inches/4 cm long)
2 red bell peppers, halved and seeded
2 yellow bell peppers, halved and seeded
1 fennel bulb, cut lengthwise into ½-inch (1 cm) thick slices
2 leeks, cut in half lengthwise
½ pound (250 g) shiitake mushrooms, stemmed (9 large caps)
  Olive oil
  Salt and pepper
¼ cup (50 mL) black olives

Vinaigrette: In large bowl, gradually whisk oil into vinegar. Whisk in basil, sage and rosemary.

Salad: Add navy beans to vinaigrette and stir to coat.

Cook green beans in large saucepan of boiling water for 3 to 5 minutes or until tender-crisp; drain. Immediately rinse under cold running water; drain well and add to navy bean mixture.

Rub red and yellow bell pepper halves, fennel slices, leeks and mushroom caps with oil. Place peppers, fennel and leeks on greased barbecue grill over medium-high heat. Cook for 12 to 15 minutes or until tender, adding mushrooms during last 8 minutes of cooking time, turning vegetables once.

Immediately put peppers in bowl and cover tightly with plastic wrap; let stand for 20 minutes to loosen skins. Peel and cut into 1-inch (2.5 cm) strips. Chop fennel and leeks. Cut mushrooms into ¼-inch (5 mm) strips.

Set aside some red pepper strips for garnish. Add fennel, leeks, mushrooms and remaining red pepper strips to bean mixture; stir to combine. Add salt and pepper to taste. Transfer to platter and sprinkle with olives.

Tips:

• *If you have the time, consider cooking your own navy beans.*
Not only will you save money, the beans will be even whiter in colour and have a fresher taste. You'll need 3 cups (750 mL) cooked beans.
About 1½ cups (375 mL) of dried beans will yield about 3 cups (750 mL) cooked beans.

• *Go ahead and substitute other grilled vegetables — such as ¼-inch (5 mm) slices red onion for leeks and other large mushrooms for shiitakes.*

• *If desired, line serving platter with fresh arugula and drizzle with olive oil. Mound bean salad mixture on top.*

Makes 6 servings. PER SERVING: 310 cal, 10 g pro, 14 g fat, 39 g carb.

Moroccan Couscous Salad

Vinaigrette

¼	cup (50 mL) fresh lemon juice
½	teaspoon (2 mL) each salt and pepper
⅓	cup (75 mL) olive oil
2	garlic cloves, minced
3	tablespoons (45 mL) chopped fresh basil
½	teaspoon (2 mL) dried oregano leaves

Salad

1¾	cups (425 mL) water
2	tablespoons (30 mL) fresh lemon juice
¼	teaspoon (1 mL) salt
1½	cups (375 mL) regular (Moroccan) couscous
1	cup (250 mL) grape or cherry tomatoes, quartered
1	cup (250 mL) crumbled feta cheese
½	cup (125 mL) thinly sliced red onion
⅓	cup (75 mL) kalamata olives, pitted and halved
1	(170 mL) jar marinated artichoke hearts, drained and halved
4	tablespoons (60 mL) chopped fresh parsley
	Salt and pepper

Vinaigrette: In small bowl, whisk together lemon juice, salt and pepper. Gradually whisk in oil. Whisk in garlic, basil and oregano.

Salad: In large saucepan, bring water, lemon juice and ¼ teaspoon (1 mL) salt to a boil. Stir in couscous; cover and remove from heat. Let stand for 5 minutes. Transfer couscous to large bowl and fluff with fork; let cool for about 15 minutes, fluffing with a fork frequently.

Add tomatoes, cheese, onion, olives, artichokes and parsley to couscous; stir to mix. Whisk vinaigrette and drizzle over salad; toss to coat. Add salt and pepper to taste. Transfer to platter.

Makes 6 servings. PER SERVING: 465 cal, 14 g pro, 26 g fat, 47 g carb.

Spicy Noodle Salad

Vinaigrette

3	tablespoons (45 mL) fresh lime juice
3	tablespoons (45 mL) mirin (sweet rice wine)
3	tablespoons (45 mL) soy sauce
1¼	teaspoons (6 mL) granulated sugar
¾	teaspoon (4 mL) hot chili paste
2	tablespoons (30 mL) dark sesame oil
¼	cup (50 mL) finely chopped shallots
1	tablespoon (15 mL) finely chopped fresh ginger
1	small garlic clove, minced

Salad

1	(300 g) package fresh thin egg noodles or ½ pound (250 g) dried thin egg noodles
¼	pound (125 g) snow peas, trimmed (1 cup/250 mL)
½	cup (125 mL) sliced green onions
2	large carrots, julienned or grated
¼	English cucumber, halved lengthwise and sliced thin
½	cup (125 mL) coarsely chopped, roasted unsalted peanuts, divided (optional)
½	cup (125 mL) coarsely chopped fresh cilantro, divided
	Salt and pepper

Vinaigrette: In small bowl, whisk together lime juice, mirin, soy sauce, sugar and chili paste. Gradually whisk in oil. Whisk in shallot, ginger and garlic.

Salad: Cook fresh noodles in large pot of boiling salted water for 2 minutes or until tender, adding peas during last 1 minute of cooking time; drain. Immediately rinse noodles and peas under cold running water; drain well and put in large bowl. (If using dried noodles, prepare according to package directions, adding peas for last minute of cooking.)

Add onions, carrots, cucumber, ¼ cup (50 mL) each of peanuts and cilantro to noodles and peas.

Whisk vinaigrette and drizzle over salad; toss to coat. Add salt and pepper to taste. Transfer to platter. Sprinkle with remaining cilantro and peanuts.

Tips:

• *Make ahead: Prepare vinaigrette and vegetables (except cucumber) and refrigerate overnight. Chop peanuts; set aside. About an hour before serving, remove vinaigrette from refrigerator and let come to room temperature. Cook noodles and snow peas, slice cucumber and whisk vinaigrette; assemble salad and serve.*
• *Add cold cooked shrimp for a main course meal.*
• *Mirin is a sweet Japanese cooking wine made from rice. It's sold in most supermarkets and Asian grocery stores. Once opened, keep refrigerated.*
• *The term julienne means cutting foods into matchstick strips.*
• *For some, the pungent flavour of cilantro (also called Chinese parsley) is an acquired taste — if desired, substitute curly leaf or Italian (flat-leaf) parsley.*

Makes 8 servings. PER SERVING: 166 cal, 5 g pro, 9 g fat, 18 g carb.

Israeli Couscous and Lentil Salad

Vinaigrette
6	tablespoons (90 mL) fresh lemon juice
½	teaspoon (2 mL) liquid honey
¼	teaspoon (1 mL) ground cumin
¼	teaspoon (1 mL) each salt and pepper
6	tablespoons (90 mL) olive oil
1	garlic clove, minced

Salad
1	cup (250 mL) organic green or French lentils (lentils du Puy), rinsed and drained
1¾	cups (425 mL) Israeli couscous
½	cup (125 mL) chopped red onion
1	small red bell pepper, cut into thin strips
½	cup (125 mL) slivered dried apricots
⅓	cup (75 mL) raisins
½	cup (125 mL) unsalted natural pistachios or cashews
½	cup (125 mL) chopped fresh cilantro
	Salt and pepper
8	Lemon wedges

Vinaigrette: In small bowl, whisk together lemon juice, honey, cumin, salt and pepper. Gradually whisk in oil. Whisk in garlic.

Salad: In medium saucepan, bring 6 cups (1.5 L) water to a boil over high heat. Add lentils, reduce heat to medium-low and simmer, partially covered, for 20 minutes or until tender but not mushy; drain. Immediately rinse lentils under cold running water; drain well and put in large bowl.

Meanwhile, cook couscous in large pot of boiling water for 10 minutes or until tender; drain. (Cooking time may vary because the size of Israeli couscous varies). Immediately rinse couscous under cold running water; drain well and add to lentils. Add onion, bell pepper, apricots, raisins, pistachios and cilantro.

Whisk vinaigrette and drizzle over salad; toss to coat. Add salt and pepper to taste. Transfer to platter. Garnish with lemon wedges.

Tips:

• *Maximize the flavour of cumin by roasting seeds before grinding. Buying ground cumin may save time, but for superior flavour, start with whole seeds and roast them yourself. Use a small, dry heavy frypan over medium-high heat; add seeds and roast for 1 to 2 minutes or until fragrant and just slightly darkened, shaking pan constantly. Grind seeds in mortar and pestle, or in clean coffee grinder or spice grinder. Store ground cumin in clean spice jar away from heat and direct light.*

• *Add cold ham, chicken or shrimp for a main course meal.*

Makes 8 servings. PER SERVING: 397 cal, 12 g pro, 15 g fat, 56 g carb.

Roasted Asparagus and Israeli Couscous Salad

Vinaigrette

¼	cup (50 mL) white wine vinegar
¼	teaspoon (1 mL) liquid honey
¼	teaspoon (1 mL) salt
⅛	teaspoon (0.5 mL) pepper
¼	cup (50 mL) olive oil
1	small garlic clove, minced

Salad

1	pound (500 g) asparagus, trimmed
2	teaspoons (10 mL) olive oil
	Salt and pepper
1¾	cups (425 mL) Israeli couscous
¼	pound (125 g) snow peas, trimmed (1 cup/250 mL)
½	cup (125 mL) chopped red onion
3	tablespoons (45 mL) chopped, drained sun-dried tomatoes (packed in oil)
¼	cup (50 mL) pine nuts, toasted
½	cup (125 mL) chopped fresh Italian (flat-leaf) parsley

Vinaigrette: In small bowl, whisk together vinegar, honey, salt and pepper. Gradually whisk in oil. Whisk in garlic.

Salad: Toss asparagus in oil and place, in single layer, on rimmed baking sheet. Bake at 500 F (260 C) for 5 to 8 minutes, turning once. Lightly sprinkle with salt and pepper. Let cool to room temperature, then cut asparagus into 2-inch (5 cm) pieces.

Cook couscous in large pot of boiling salted water for 10 minutes or until tender, adding peas during last 1 minute of cooking time; drain. (Cooking time may vary because the size of Israeli couscous varies.) Immediately rinse couscous and peas under cold running water; drain well. Cut peas in half crosswise.

In large bowl, combine couscous, peas, asparagus, onion, sun-dried tomatoes, pine nuts and parsley.

Whisk vinaigrette and drizzle over salad; toss to coat. Add salt and pepper to taste. Transfer to platter.

Tips:

• *Couscous varies in size from the minuscule Moroccan instant granular couscous to the slightly larger Israeli couscous. In its more familiar Moroccan form, it is the smallest of all pastas — all it needs is a quick soak in boiling water or stock before serving. Israeli couscous, sometimes called pearl or toasted couscous (about the size of peppercorns or pearl tapioca) is chewier than the instant. Cook Israeli couscous like any other pasta, in boiling salted water for 10 minutes or until tender. If you can't find this trendy toothsome couscous substitute orzo (rice-shaped pasta).*

• *Make ahead: Assemble salad without cooked snow peas and asparagus, cover tightly and refrigerate overnight. Put cooked snow peas and asparagus in separate bowl, cover tightly and refrigerate overnight. Just before serving, add snow peas and asparagus to salad. (The vegetables will lose their bright green colour if left in dressing overnight.)*

• *A 250-gram package of Israeli couscous yields about 1¾ cups (425 mL) uncooked couscous.*

• *Keep this salad recipe handy for the barbecue season — it's perfect for serving alongside grilled chicken or pork.*

Makes 8 servings. PER SERVING: 279 cal, 9 g pro, 10 g fat, 39 g carb.

Tangy Tabbouleh

Salad

1	cup (250 mL) medium bulgur
3½	cups (875 mL) boiling water
1	(398 mL) can lentils, drained and rinsed
1	cup (250 mL) diced English cucumber
1	cup (250 mL) diced seeded plum tomatoes
½	cup (125 mL) sliced green onions
1	cup (250 mL) chopped fresh Italian (flat-leaf) parsley
⅓	cup (75 mL) chopped fresh mint
	Salt and pepper
	Romaine lettuce

Vinaigrette

3	tablespoons (45 mL) fresh lemon juice
1	teaspoon (5 mL) salt
½	teaspoon (2 mL) pepper
¼	cup (50 mL) olive oil

Salad: Put bulgur in large bowl. Add boiling water; cover and let stand for 30 minutes or until tender and cool.

Pour soaked bulgur into sieve; stir and firmly press bulgur with back of large spoon to squeeze out water. Transfer to large bowl and add lentils, cucumber, tomatoes, onions, parsley and mint; toss to combine.

Vinaigrette: In small bowl, whisk together lemon juice, salt and pepper. Gradually whisk in oil. Drizzle over salad; toss to coat. Add salt and pepper to taste. *(Make ahead: Cover and refrigerate for up to 8 hours.)* Line platter with lettuce and spoon room temperature or chilled bulgur mixture in mound on top.

Tip: Do not substitute cracked wheat for bulgur wheat.

Makes 8 servings. PER SERVING: 165 cal, 6 g pro, 6 g fat, 23 g carb.

Ancient Grain Salad

Salad

½   cup (125 mL) kamut kernels
½   cup (125 mL) spelt kernels
½   cup (125 mL) drained, canned corn
½   cup (125 mL) diced red bell pepper
½   cup (125 mL) currants
2   tablespoons (30 mL) sliced green onion
    Salt and pepper

Vinaigrette

1   tablespoon (15 mL) plus 1 teaspoon (5 mL) natural rice vinegar
1¼ teaspoons (6 mL) liquid honey
¼   teaspoon (1 mL) dijon mustard
½   teaspoon (2 mL) salt
¼   teaspoon (1 mL) pepper
3   tablespoons (45 mL) olive oil
1   tablespoon (15 mL) finely chopped shallot
¾   teaspoon (4 mL) minced fresh ginger
1   tablespoon (15 mL) chopped fresh cilantro

Salad: In medium saucepan, bring 4 cups (1 L) water to a boil. Add kamut and spelt kernels; bring to a boil. Reduce heat to low, cover and simmer for about 45 minutes or until kernels are tender (kernels will still be chewy). Let kernels drain in sieve for about 1½ hours or until room temperature, stirring occasionally.

In large bowl, combine kernels, corn, bell pepper, currants and onion.

Vinaigrette: In small bowl, whisk together vinegar, honey, mustard, salt and pepper. Gradually whisk in oil. Whisk in shallot, ginger and cilantro.

Drizzle vinaigrette over salad; toss to coat. Add salt and pepper to taste. Cover tightly and refrigerate overnight or until chilled.

Tips:

• Kamut is a high-protein ancient variety of wheat that has been rediscovered recently by consumers in North America. The name kamut originated from the ancient Egyptian word for "wheat". Kamut was cultivated in Egypt about 4,000 B.C. The torpedo-shaped kernels are much larger than regular wheat kernels and have a pronounced nutty flavour and pleasant chewy texture.

• Spelt kernels are oval-shaped and red-brown in colour with a mellow nutty flavour. This wheat thrived in Europe more than 9,000 years ago, and for centuries was popular in Europe, Egypt and throughout the Mediterranean. Although difficult to find in the 1900s, it, too, has made a comeback.

• If buying in bulk, be sure kamut and spelt smell fresh and nutty — they can become rancid. Store in an airtight container in freezer.

Makes 4 servings. PER SERVING: 315 cal, 9 g pro, 12 g fat, 48 g carb.

Heirloom Tomato Salad (recipe on following page)

Mainly VEGGIES

Heirloom Tomato Salad

Tapenade vinaigrette

¼	cup (50 mL) olive oil
2	teaspoons (10 mL) red wine vinegar
1	tablespoon (15 mL) tapenade
2	tablespoons (30 mL) chopped fresh Italian (flat-leaf) parsley
1	tablespoon (15 mL) chopped fresh basil

Salad

4	large red heirloom or other tomatoes, sliced
2	small orange tomatoes, cut into wedges
2	small yellow tomatoes, cut into wedges
1	cup (250 mL) grape or cherry tomatoes, halved
½	cup (125 mL) chopped red onion
1	cup (250 mL) crumbled feta cheese
	Salt and pepper

Tapenade Vinaigrette: In small bowl, gradually whisk oil into vinegar. Whisk in tapenade, parsley and basil.

Salad: Arrange red tomato slices, overlapping slightly, on platter. Place orange and yellow tomato wedges, and grape tomatoes on top. Sprinkle with onion and cheese.

Whisk vinaigrette and drizzle over salad. Add salt and pepper to taste.

Tip: Tapenade is a thick olive paste, made from a variety of high-intensity ingredients such as capers, anchovies, ripe olives, olive oil, lemon juice and seasonings. It's available fresh or in jars.

Makes 8 servings. PER SERVING: 184 cal, 6 g pro, 14 g fat, 9 g carb.

Harvest Tomato Salad

4   large tomatoes, sliced
3   tablespoons (45 mL) extra-virgin olive oil
1   tablespoon (15 mL) balsamic vinegar
        Salt and pepper
2   tablespoons (30 mL) chopped fresh basil or oregano

Arrange tomato slices, overlapping slightly, on platter. Drizzle with oil and vinegar. Sprinkle with salt and pepper to taste. Sprinkle with basil.

Tips:

• *The ultimate in simplicity, this salad requires vine-ripened tomatoes, good quality balsamic vinegar and fresh herbs.*
• *To make the well-known Italian salad called insalata alla caprese, thinly slice mozzarella balls (preferably buffalo milk mozzarella) and layer between juicy tomato slices. Or, try scattering mini boccocini over top. Mini boccocini can be bought either plain or marinated in oil with fresh herbs.*

Makes 4 servings. PER SERVING: 119 cal, 1 g pro, 11 g fat, 6 g carb.

Potatoes with Lemon Vinaigrette

Salad

2   pounds (1 kg) small nugget potatoes (unpeeled)
½   pound (250 g) sugar snap peas, trimmed (2 cups/500 mL), optional
2   tablespoons (30 mL) chopped fresh chives or baby dill
         Salt and pepper

Vinaigrette

3   tablespoons (45 mL) fresh lemon juice
1   teaspoon (5 mL) dijon mustard
½   teaspoon (2 mL) each salt and pepper
3   tablespoons (45 mL) extra-virgin olive oil
1   garlic clove, minced

Salad: Scrub potatoes. Cook in large pot of boiling water for 15 to 20 minutes or until just tender; drain. Let potatoes cool to room temperature (about 1 hour); put in large bowl.

Cook peas in large saucepan of boiling water for 1 minute or until tender-crisp; drain. Immediately rinse under cold running water; drain well. Add peas and chives to potatoes.

Vinaigrette: In small bowl, whisk together lemon juice, mustard, salt and pepper. Gradually whisk in oil. Whisk in garlic. Drizzle over salad; toss gently to coat. Add salt and pepper to taste. Transfer to platter. Serve at room temperature.

Tip: Nugget potatoes are sweet-tasting, knobbly little potatoes (with their wisps of skin still attached) that come to market in late spring and early summer. Once they disappear from stores, any small new potato will do.

Makes 6 servings. PER SERVING: 201 cal, 5 g pro, 7 g fat, 31 g carb.

Warm Nugget Potato Toss

Salad

2	pounds (1 kg) small nugget potatoes (unpeeled)
⅓	cup (75 mL) slivered fresh basil, divided
	Salt and pepper
½	cup (125 mL) grated asiago cheese

Vinaigrette

1	tablespoon (15 mL) balsamic vinegar
1	teaspoon (5 mL) dijon mustard
¼	teaspoon (1 mL) each salt and pepper
¼	cup (50 mL) olive oil from bottled sun-dried tomatoes
¼	cup (50 mL) slivered, drained sun-dried tomatoes (packed in oil)
1	garlic clove, minced

Salad: Scrub potatoes. Cook in large pot of boiling water for 15 to 20 minutes or until just tender; drain, reserving 1 tablespoon (15 mL) potato water for vinaigrette. Put potatoes in large bowl.

Vinaigrette: In small bowl, whisk together reserved potato water, vinegar, mustard, salt and pepper. Gradually whisk in oil. Whisk in sun-dried tomatoes and garlic. Drizzle over warm potatoes; toss gently to coat. Add ¼ cup (50 mL) basil; toss gently. Add salt and pepper to taste. Transfer to platter; sprinkle with cheese and remaining basil. Serve warm.

Tips:

• *To sliver fresh basil, stack and roll leaves tightly, cut crosswise into thin slivers.*

• *Asiago cheese is a sharp-tasting cow's milk cheese with a rich nutty flavour. In a pinch, old white cheddar cheese can be substituted.*

Makes 6 servings. PER SERVING: 255 cal, 6 g pro, 11 g fat, 34 g carb.

Warm Southern Potato Toss

2	pounds (1 kg) small nugget potatoes (unpeeled)
3	tablespoons (45 mL) olive oil
1	tablespoon (15 mL) red wine vinegar
¾	cup (175 mL) toasted pecan halves, divided
1	garlic clove, minced
	Salt and pepper
½	cup (125 mL) chopped fresh parsley, divided
⅓	cup (75 mL) shaved parmesan cheese

Scrub potatoes. Cook in large pot of boiling water for 15 to 20 minutes or until just tender; drain, reserving 1 tablespoon (15 mL) potato water. Put potatoes in large bowl.

In blender or food processor, blend reserved potato water, oil, vinegar, ¼ cup (50 mL) pecans, garlic and ¼ teaspoon (1 mL) each of salt and pepper.

Add blended pecan dressing, ¼ cup (50 mL) parsley and remaining pecans to warm potatoes; toss gently to coat.

Add salt and pepper to taste. Transfer to platter; sprinkle with cheese and remaining parsley. Serve warm.

Tip: *To shave parmesan cheese, use a vegetable peeler to remove delicate paper-thin shards of parmesan cheese from a block of good quality Parmigiano-Reggiano.*

Makes 6 servings. PER SERVING: 305 cal, 7 g pro, 18 g fat, 32 g carb.

Tricolour New Potato Salad

Salad

4   (¼-inch/5 mm thick) slices sweet onion

      Olive oil

2   pounds (1 kg) small new potatoes (unpeeled, combination of red, yellow and blue)

      Salt and pepper

1   tablespoon (15 mL) chopped fresh parsley

Vinaigrette

2   tablespoons (30 mL) white balsamic vinegar

1   tablespoon (15 mL) fresh lemon juice

1½   teaspoons (7 mL) grainy mustard

½   teaspoon (2 mL) salt

¼   teaspoon (1 mL) pepper

3   tablespoons (45 mL) olive oil

2   garlic cloves, minced

Salad: Place onion slices on greased broiler pan and brush with oil. Broil 3 inches (7 cm) from heat source for 6 minutes. Turn slices over and brush with oil; broil for 6 minutes or until tender. Let slices cool, then chop.

Scrub potatoes and cut any large ones in half. Cook in large pot of boiling water for 15 to 20 minutes or until just tender; drain. Let potatoes cool to room temperature (about 1 hour); cut into small chunks and put in large bowl. Add chopped onions.

Vinaigrette: In small bowl, whisk together vinegar, lemon juice, mustard, salt and pepper. Gradually whisk in oil. Whisk in garlic. Drizzle over salad; toss gently to coat. Let stand for 3 minutes, tossing occasionally. Add salt and pepper to taste. Transfer to platter and sprinkle with parsley. Serve at room temperature.

Makes 6 servings. PER SERVING: 143 cal, 4 g pro, 2 g fat, 29 g carb.

Creamy Nugget Potato Salad

Salad

2	pounds (1 kg) small nugget potatoes (unpeeled)
½	cup (125 mL) thinly sliced radishes
	Salt and pepper
	Paprika, optional

Dressing

½	cup (125 mL) light sour cream
¼	cup (50 mL) light mayonnaise
2	tablespoons (30 mL) buttermilk (1.5 per cent M.F.)
¼	cup (50 mL) finely sliced green onions
¼	cup (50 mL) finely chopped fresh Italian (flat-leaf) parsley
¾	teaspoon (4 mL) salt
½	teaspoon (2 mL) pepper

Salad: Scrub potatoes. Cook in large pot of boiling water for 15 to 20 minutes or until just tender; drain. Let potatoes cool to room temperature (about 1 hour); cut into quarters and put in large bowl with radishes.

Dressing: In small bowl, whisk together sour cream, mayonnaise, buttermilk, onions, parsley, salt and pepper.

Drizzle dressing over salad; toss gently to coat. Add salt and pepper to taste. Sprinkle lightly with paprika. Cover and refrigerate until chilled.

Tip: *We've trimmed the fat but not the flavour in this salad by using light sour cream and light mayonnaise. If you use regular sour cream and regular mayonnaise, each serving will have an additional 5 grams of fat and another 42 calories.*

Makes 6 servings. PER SERVING: 174 cal, 5 g pro, 4 g fat, 31 g carb.

Roasted Beet and Walnut Salad

Vinaigrette

1	tablespoon (15 mL) cider vinegar
¼	teaspoon (1 mL) each salt and pepper
3	tablespoons (45 mL) walnut oil
1	tablespoon (15 mL) finely chopped shallot

Salad

5	(2½ inches/6 cm in diameter) beets (1¼ pounds/625 g total)
1	tablespoon (15 mL) olive oil
4	cups (1 L) torn mixed salad greens
½	cup (125 mL) walnuts, toasted
¼	cup (50 mL) unripened soft goat cheese, cut into small pieces
	Salt and pepper

Vinaigrette: In small bowl, whisk together vinegar, salt and pepper. Gradually whisk in oil. Whisk in shallot.

Salad: Peel beets and cut each beet into 8 wedges; put in bowl. Drizzle oil over beets; toss to coat. Put beets in 13x9-inch (33x23 cm) baking pan. Cover tightly with foil and bake at 350 F (180 C) for 40 minutes. Uncover and bake for 10 minutes or until tender. Remove beets from pan and let cool to room temperature. *(Make ahead: Roasted beets can be covered tightly and refrigerated overnight. Let come to room temperature before assembling salad.)*

Place an equal portion of greens on each of 4 large plates. Arrange an equal portion of beets on top of each plate of greens. Sprinkle each serving with an equal portion of walnuts and goat cheese. Whisk vinaigrette and drizzle each salad with about 1 tablespoon (15 mL) vinaigrette. Sprinkle with salt and pepper to taste.

Tip: Olive oil can be substituted for walnut oil.

Makes 4 servings. PER SERVING: 349 cal, 10 g pro, 28 g fat, 19 g carb.

Corn and Tomatillo Salad

Vinaigrette

1	tablespoon (15 mL) balsamic vinegar
¼	teaspoon (1 mL) each salt and pepper
2	tablespoons (30 mL) olive oil
1	to 2 teaspoons (5 to 10 mL) minced, canned chipotle pepper in adobo sauce
1	garlic clove, minced

Salad

4	large ears corn, kernels removed
4	tomatillos, husked and diced
½	orange bell pepper, diced
½	red bell pepper, diced
2	tablespoons (30 mL) chopped, drained sun-dried tomatoes (packed in oil)
1	green onion, sliced
2	tablespoons (30 mL) chopped fresh cilantro
	Salt and pepper

Vinaigrette: In small bowl, whisk together vinegar, salt and pepper. Gradually whisk in oil. Whisk in chipotle pepper and garlic.

Salad: In medium saucepan, cook corn kernels in boiling water for 2 minutes or until tender-crisp; drain. Immediately rinse under cold running water; drain well. In large bowl, combine tomatillos, orange and red bell peppers, sun-dried tomatoes, onion, cilantro and corn.

Whisk vinaigrette and drizzle over salad; toss to coat. Add salt and pepper to taste.

Tips:

• When fresh corn is not in season or if you would like to reduce the preparation time, then simply substitute 2 drained (341 mL) cans whole kernel corn for the 4 large ears.

• Chipotle peppers are dried, smoked jalapeno peppers. Look for small cans of these whole peppers packed in a rich mahogany-red sauce called adobo — a mixture of onions, tomatoes, vinegar and spices. Use this fiery mixture judiciously to add a hot smoky flavour to food. A can usually contains more chipotle peppers than can be used at any one time — freeze leftovers for future use. Transfer peppers and sauce into a resealable freezer bag, separating peppers slightly so that it will be easy to break off the desired amount when necessary, rather than thawing the whole mass. Look for chipotles in adobo at specialty food stores or large supermarkets.

• Tomatillos, sometimes called Mexican green tomatoes, are about the same size as cherry tomatoes and have a lemony-herbal flavour. They come enclosed in a thin papery husk which is easily peeled off. Store in paper bag in refrigerator for up to 3 weeks.

Makes 4 servings. PER SERVING: 262 cal, 8 g pro, 10 g fat, 44 g carb.

Old-Fashioned Cucumber Salad

1	English cucumber, sliced thin (3 cups/750 mL)
⅓	cup (75 mL) water
3	tablespoons (45 mL) white vinegar
2	tablespoons (30 mL) granulated sugar
¼	teaspoon (1 mL) salt
⅛	teaspoon (0.5 mL) white pepper
1	tablespoon (15 mL) finely chopped fresh chives, optional
1	tablespoon (15 mL) chopped fresh baby dill

Put cucumber slices in medium-size heatproof bowl.

In small saucepan, combine water, vinegar, sugar, salt and pepper. Place over medium heat and bring to a simmer, stirring until sugar dissolves. Remove from heat and pour over cucumber slices. Let stand at room temperature until cool, stirring frequently. Cover and refrigerate overnight, stirring occasionally.

When ready to serve, stir in chives and dill. With slotted spoon, transfer to serving bowl.

Tips:

• *Be sure to look for tender fresh baby dill, not the coarser mature dill used for pickling.*
• *Black pepper can be substituted for the white pepper.*

Makes 6 servings. PER SERVING: 24 cal, 0 g pro, 0 g fat, 6 g carb.

Asian Coleslaw

Vinaigrette

2	tablespoons (30 mL) fresh lime juice
2	teaspoons (10 mL) natural rice vinegar
4	teaspoons (20 mL) granulated sugar
	Pinch pepper
2	tablespoons (30 mL) vegetable oil
2	garlic cloves, minced
1	serrano pepper, seeded and minced

Salad

2	cups (500 mL) bean sprouts
2	cups (500 mL) finely shredded savoy cabbage
½	cup (125 mL) thinly sliced sweet onion
½	cup (125 mL) thinly sliced small radishes
½	small red bell pepper, sliced very thin
1	tablespoon (15 mL) chopped fresh cilantro
	Salt and pepper

Vinaigrette: In small bowl, whisk together lime juice, vinegar, sugar and pepper. Gradually whisk in oil. Whisk in garlic and serrano pepper.

Salad: In large bowl, combine bean sprouts, cabbage, onion, radishes, bell pepper and cilantro. Whisk vinaigrette and drizzle over salad; toss to coat. Add salt and pepper to taste.

Tips:

• *Savoy cabbage has green crinkly leaves. It has a slightly softer texture and milder flavour than the common green variety of cabbage.*

• *To slice onion, cut in half lengthwise. Lay onion half, cut side down, and slice crosswise into very thin slices.*

Makes 4 servings. PER SERVING: 126 cal, 3 g pro, 7 g fat, 15 g carb.

Coleslaw with Light Creamy Dressing

Salad

2½   cups (625 mL) shredded green cabbage

2   green onions, sliced

1   large carrot, grated

¼   cup (50 mL) dried cranberries

    Salt and pepper

Dressing

¼   cup (50 mL) light mayonnaise

¼   cup (50 mL) light sour cream

1   tablespoon (15 mL) cider vinegar

1   tablespoon (15 mL) seasoned rice vinegar

1½   teaspoons (7 mL) fresh lemon juice

1¼   teaspoons (6 mL) granulated sugar

½   teaspoon (2 mL) dijon mustard

¼   teaspoon (1 mL) each salt and pepper

⅛   teaspoon (0.5 mL) celery seeds (optional)

Salad: In large bowl, combine cabbage, onions, carrot and cranberries.

Dressing: In small bowl, whisk together mayonnaise, sour cream, cider vinegar, rice vinegar, lemon juice, sugar, mustard, salt, pepper and celery seeds until blended. Drizzle over salad; toss to coat. Add salt and pepper to taste. *(Make ahead: Cover and refrigerate for up to 1 day.)*

Tip: *For convenience, use packaged, washed and ready-to-eat coleslaw. Substitute 2½ cups (625 mL) coleslaw for the shredded cabbage.*

Makes 4 servings. PER SERVING: 98 cal, 2 g pro, 5 g fat, 13 g carb.

Grilled Vegetable Salad

Vinaigrette

2	tablespoons (30 mL) balsamic vinegar
1½	teaspoons (7 mL) dijon mustard
¼	teaspoon (1 mL) each salt and pepper
¼	cup (50 mL) olive oil
1	garlic clove, minced
1	tablespoon (15 mL) finely chopped shallot

Salad

½	pound (250 g) asparagus, trimmed
1	small red onion, cut into ¼-inch (5 mm) thick slices
2	Japanese eggplants, cut diagonally into ½-inch (1 cm) thick slices
1	red bell pepper, cut lengthwise into quarters
	Olive oil
	Salt and pepper
8	cups (2 L) torn mixed sturdy salad greens

Vinaigrette: In small bowl, whisk together vinegar, mustard, salt and pepper. Gradually whisk in oil. Whisk in garlic and shallot.

Salad: Lightly brush asparagus, onion, eggplants and bell pepper with oil. Place on greased barbecue grill over medium-high heat; cook for 8 to 15 minutes or until browned and tender, turning and brushing occasionally with oil. (Asparagus will take 6 to 10 minutes. Onion, eggplant and bell pepper, 12 to 15 minutes.) Let vegetables cool to room temperature. Cut asparagus into bite-size pieces. Peel red pepper; cut into small pieces. Sprinkle vegetables with salt and pepper to taste.

Put greens in large bowl; add vegetables and toss. Whisk vinaigrette and drizzle over salad; toss to coat.

Tip: Skewer onion slices with a toothpick to secure them while grilling.

Makes 8 servings. PER SERVING: 78 cal, 2 g pro, 6 g fat, 5 g carb.

Asparagus with Lemon Vinaigrette

Vinaigrette

1	tablespoon (15 mL) fresh lemon juice
¾	teaspoon (4 mL) grainy mustard
¼	teaspoon (1 mL) salt
⅛	teaspoon (0.5 mL) pepper
¼	cup (50 mL) extra-virgin olive oil
1	tablespoon (15 mL) finely chopped shallot
1	teaspoon (5 mL) finely grated lemon zest
1	small yellow or orange bell pepper, roasted and chopped coarse

Salad

3	pounds (1.5 kg) asparagus, trimmed
	Salt and pepper

Vinaigrette: In small bowl, whisk together lemon juice, mustard, salt and pepper. Gradually whisk in oil. Whisk in shallot and lemon zest.

Salad: In large pot of boiling salted water, cook asparagus for about 3 minutes or until tender-crisp. Drain well and transfer to platter. Sprinkle lightly with salt and pepper. Whisk vinaigrette and stir in bell pepper; drizzle over asparagus.

Tips:

• *To remove tough ends of asparagus, hold centre of stalk with one hand, and root end of stalk with your other; bend asparagus until it snaps at the point where it gives most easily. Discard the short piece of tough stalk.*

• *There are several brands of grainy mustard, some stronger in flavour than others. We used Grey brand prepared old style mustard, if you use a different brand, add mustard to taste.*

Makes 8 servings. PER SERVING: 97 cal, 6 g pro, 6 g fat, 8 g carb.

Roasted Asparagus with Fig Balsamic Vinaigrette

Vinaigrette

2   tablespoons (30 mL) fig or regular balsamic vinegar
⅛   teaspoon (0.5 mL) each salt and pepper
3   tablespoons (45 mL) olive oil
1   small garlic clove, minced
1   tablespoon (15 mL) finely chopped shallot
2   tablespoons (30 mL) chopped fresh Italian (flat-leaf) parsley

Salad

1½   pounds (750 g) asparagus, trimmed
1   tablespoon (15 mL) olive oil
     Salt and pepper
¼   cup (50 mL) shaved parmesan cheese

Vinaigrette: In small bowl, whisk together vinegar, salt and pepper. Gradually whisk in oil. Whisk in garlic, shallot and parsley.

Salad: Toss asparagus in oil and place, in single layer, on rimmed baking sheet. Bake at 500 F (260 C) for 5 to 8 minutes, turning once. Lightly sprinkle with salt and pepper. Transfer to platter.

Whisk vinaigrette and drizzle over asparagus. Top with shaved parmesan.

Tips:

• Aromatic Italian (flat-leaf) parsley has a fresh, peppery taste and is stronger in flavour than the mild curly-leaf parsley.
• During barbecue season, grill asparagus. Lightly brush asparagus spears with olive oil; place on greased grill over medium-high heat. Cook for 6 to 10 minutes or until tender-crisp, turning occasionally.

Makes 4 servings. PER SERVING: 183 cal, 7 g pro, 16 g fat, 5 g carb.

Creamy Broccoli and Grape Salad

Salad

4   cups (1 L) small broccoli florets
1   cup (250 mL) seedless green grapes, halved
1   cup (250 mL) seedless red grapes, halved
½   cup (125 mL) finely sliced celery
¼   cup (50 mL) sliced green onions
½   cup (125 mL) sliced natural almonds, toasted
5   slices bacon, cooked crisp and crumbled
    Salt and pepper

Dressing

½   cup (125 mL) light mayonnaise
¼   cup (50 mL) light sour cream
1   tablespoon (15 mL) pure white vinegar
2   tablespoons (30 mL) granulated sugar
¼   teaspoon (1 mL) pepper
⅛   teaspoon (0.5 mL) salt

Salad: Cook broccoli in large saucepan of boiling water for 1 minute; drain. Immediately rinse under cold running water; drain well and pat with paper towels to remove excess moisture. Put broccoli in large bowl. Add green and red grapes, celery, onions, almonds and bacon.

Dressing: In small bowl, whisk together mayonnaise, sour cream, vinegar, sugar, pepper and salt; add to salad and stir to combine. Add salt and pepper to taste.

Tip: *Substitute 2 ounces (60 g) coarsely chopped prosciutto for bacon. In medium-size heavy frypan, heat ½ teaspoon (2 mL) vegetable oil over medium heat. Add prosciutto and saute for 3 minutes or until crisp; let cool.*

Makes 5 servings. PER SERVING: 234 cal, 11 g pro, 13 g fat, 23 g carb.

Edamame Salad

Vinaigrette

2	tablespoons (30 mL) natural rice vinegar
2	teaspoons (10 mL) granulated sugar
¼	teaspoon (1 mL) salt
1	tablespoon (15 mL) vegetable oil
⅛	teaspoon (0.5 mL) crushed dried hot red pepper

Salad

3	cups (750 mL) frozen shelled edamame
½	small red bell pepper, diced
2	green onions, sliced
	Salt

Vinaigrette: In small bowl, whisk together vinegar, sugar and salt. Gradually whisk in oil. Whisk in dried red pepper.

Salad: Cook edamame in large saucepan of boiling salted water for 3 to 5 minutes or until tender; drain. Immediately rinse under cold running water; drain well and put in large bowl. Add bell pepper and onions.

Whisk vinaigrette and drizzle over salad; toss to coat. Add salt to taste.

Tips:

• The Japanese name for fresh green soy beans is edamame. Although it's difficult to find fresh beans, they're readily available frozen, either shelled or in their pods.

• One (500 g) package of frozen shelled edamame yields about 3 cups (750 mL).

Makes 6 servings. PER SERVING: 164 cal, 12 g pro, 8 g fat, 13 g carb.

Fresh Fruit with a Hint of Maple

Salad

2   cups (500 mL) thickly sliced strawberries
4   kiwifruit, cut in half lengthwise and sliced thin
2   navel oranges, sectioned
1   small cantaloupe, cut into balls or bite-size pieces
1   small honeydew melon, cut into balls or bite-size pieces
1   large mango, cubed

Dressing

⅓   cup (75 mL) fresh orange juice
¼   cup (50 mL) maple syrup
1   tablespoon (15 mL) fresh lemon juice

Salad: In large bowl, combine strawberries, kiwifruit, oranges, cantaloupe, melon and mango.

Dressing: In small bowl, whisk together orange juice, maple syrup and lemon juice. Add to fruit; stir to coat. *(Make ahead: Refrigerate for up to 8 hours.)*

Tips:

• *Add or substitute your favourite fruit — pineapple, papaya, star fruit (carambola).*
• *For a stunning presentation, combine colourful bite-size chunks of fresh fruit in a large, clear bowl.*

Makes 8 servings. PER SERVING: 115 cal, 2 g pro, 1 g fat, 29 g carb.

Mixed Fruit with Ginger Dressing

Salad

1	cup (250 mL) honeydew melon balls
1	cup (250 mL) sliced strawberries
2	kiwifruit, cut into small wedges
1	mango, cubed
	French vanilla yogurt
	Fresh mint sprigs

Dressing

2	tablespoons (30 mL) pineapple juice
1	tablespoon (15 mL) ginger marmalade
2	teaspoons (10 mL) fresh lime juice
1	teaspoon (5 mL) liquid honey

Salad: In large bowl, combine melon, strawberries, kiwifruit and mango.

Dressing: In small microwaveable bowl, combine pineapple juice, marmalade, lime juice and honey. Microwave on High for 30 seconds or until mixture is warm. Pour over fruit mixture, cover and refrigerate until chilled, stirring occasionally. *(Make ahead: Refrigerate for up to 8 hours.)*

Just before serving, spoon fruit mixture into bowls. Top each serving with a dollop of yogurt and a mint sprig.

Tip: To cube the flesh of a mango, hold it so the narrow side faces you, stem end up. Make one vertical cut about ½ inch (1 cm) to the right of the stem, just clearing the pit in the centre, and another ½ inch (1 cm) to the left of the stem. Cut flesh of each half into squares being careful not to cut through the skin, then press skin so flesh pops outward. Using sharp knife, slice flesh from skin.

Makes 4 servings. PER SERVING: 91 cal, 2 g pro, 1 g fat, 21 g carb.

Orange, Olive and Fennel Salad

Vinaigrette

2½   tablespoons (37 mL) white balsamic vinegar
¼   teaspoon (1 mL) each salt and pepper
½   cup (125 mL) olive oil
2   tablespoons (30 mL) chopped fennel fronds
1   tablespoon (15 mL) finely grated fresh ginger

Salad

2   small fennel bulbs (1 pound/500 g total)
3   large navel oranges
½   small red onion, sliced thin
½   cup (125 mL) nicoise or Cretan olives
      Salt and pepper

Vinaigrette: In small bowl, whisk together vinegar, salt and pepper. Gradually whisk in oil. Whisk in fennel fronds and ginger.

Salad: Cut fennel in half lengthwise; core and cut crosswise into very thin slices. Arrange fennel on platter. Peel oranges and cut into ¼-inch (5 mm) thick slices. Arrange orange and onion slices on top of fennel. Scatter olives on top. Whisk vinaigrette and drizzle over salad. Sprinkle with salt and pepper to taste.

Tips:

• *When using whole olives that haven't been pitted, remember to alert your guests to watch out for pits.*
• *If fennel fronds (feathery foliage) have been removed from fennel bulbs, ask your green grocer if he still has them — ours did. Otherwise, omit fennel fronds from the vinaigrette.*

Makes 8 servings. PER SERVING: 195 cal, 1 g pro, 18 g fat, 10 g carb.

Mainly DRESSINGS

Fresh Berry Vinaigrette

1	cup (250 mL) fresh raspberries, blackberries or blueberries
6	tablespoons (90 mL) white balsamic vinegar
2	tablespoons (30 mL) liquid honey
1	teaspoon (5 mL) dijon mustard
½	teaspoon (2 mL) salt
¼	teaspoon (1 mL) pepper
1	cup (250 mL) vegetable oil
¼	cup (50 mL) finely chopped shallots

Puree berries in blender. Press puree through fine sieve to remove seeds or skins.

In large bowl, whisk together berry puree, vinegar, honey, mustard, salt and pepper. Gradually whisk in oil. Whisk in shallots.

Makes about 2 cups (500 mL).

Tip: For a main meal salad, arrange some thin slices of grilled chicken breast over a mix of torn sturdy salad greens and drizzle with this fresh berry vinaigrette. Don't forget to garnish with fresh berries.

Per 1-tablespoon (15 mL) serving: 64 cal, 0 g pro, 7 g fat, 2 g carb.

Maple Balsamic Vinaigrette

3	tablespoons (45 mL) balsamic vinegar
2	tablespoons (30 mL) maple syrup
4	teaspoons (20 mL) fresh lemon juice
½	teaspoon (2 mL) salt
¼	teaspoon (1 mL) pepper
½	cup (125 mL) olive oil
2	small garlic cloves, minced
1	tablespoon (15 mL) finely chopped shallot

In small bowl, whisk together vinegar, maple syrup, lemon juice, salt and pepper. Gradually whisk in oil. Whisk in garlic and shallot.

Makes about 1 cup (250 mL).

Tip: *A good quality balsamic vinegar has a rich, deep complex taste with a delicate balance of acidity and sweetness. Depending on the flavour of your brand of vinegar, you may have to adjust the amount of maple syrup.*

Per 1-tablespoon (15 mL) serving: 71 cal, 0 g pro, 7 g fat, 2 g carb.

Creamy Mustard Poppy Seed Dressing

3	tablespoons (45 mL) plus 1 teaspoon (5 mL) white wine vinegar
3	tablespoons (45 mL) liquid honey or to taste
1	tablespoon (15 mL) light mayonnaise
½	teaspoon (2 mL) dijon mustard
½	teaspoon (2 mL) each salt and pepper
¾	cup (175 mL) olive oil
1	large garlic clove, minced
1	teaspoon (5 mL) poppy seeds

In small bowl, whisk together vinegar, honey, mayonnaise, mustard, salt and pepper. Gradually whisk in oil. Whisk in garlic and poppy seeds.

Makes about 1¼ cups (300 mL).

Tip: *Poppy seeds add a little crunch and nutty flavour to this dressing. If you don't have poppy seeds on hand, simply omit them.*

Per 1-tablespoon (15 mL) serving: 84 cal, 0 g pro, 8 g fat, 3 g carb.

Tangy Lemon Vinaigrette

¼   cup (50 mL) fresh lemon juice
¾   teaspoon (4 mL) salt
¾   cup (175 mL) extra-virgin olive oil
1   small garlic clove, minced
1   tablespoon (15 mL) finely chopped fresh chives or parsley

In small bowl, whisk together lemon juice and salt. Gradually whisk in oil. Whisk in garlic and chives.

Makes about 1 cup (250 mL).

Tip: *Both heat and pressure make it easier to juice a lemon. Pierce whole lemon with sharp knife and microwave on High for about 20 seconds, then roll under palm of hand on countertop until it softens slightly; extract juice.*

Per 1-tablespoon (15 mL) serving: 89 cal, 0 g pro, 10 g fat, 0 g carb.

Index

About The Nutritional Analysis

- The approximate nutritional analysis for each recipe does not include variations or optional ingredients. Figures are rounded off.
- Abbreviations: cal = calories, pro = protein, carb = carbohydrate
- The analysis is based on the first ingredient listed where there is a choice.